The Letters of A Citizen on India Affairs

Anonymous

Anonymous

The Letters of A Citizen on India Affairs

ISBN/EAN: 9783744715676

Printed in Europe, USA, Canada, Australia, Japan

Cover: Foto ©Suzi / pixelio.de

More available books at www.hansebooks.com

L E T T E R S, &c.

L E T T E R I.

Mr. EDITOR,

I HAVE lately read two letters, addreffed to Mr. Burke, by a Major John Scott, and I find, upon enquiry, that this perfon is the agent of Mr. Haftings; and that Mr. Haftings has hitherto baffled every attempt made by Parliament, by Minifters, and by the Court of Directors, to remove him from the government of Bengal. I muft confefs to you, Mr. Editor, that I looked up to Mr. Burke, for many years, as to a fuperior being. —His eloquence, his learning, his philanthropy, and his difintereftednefs, were unqueftionable with a great majority of the nation, as well as with myfelf. His conduct in office

laft

laft year, was not, however, quite upon a par with his former profeffions, and the eagernefs with which he has purfued his own intereft, and the intereft of his relations, fince the memorable and difgraceful coalition took place, has induced me to believe that Mr. Burke is at leaft as frail a mortal as myfelf.

I know nothing of Mr. Haftings, and I believed Mr. Burke was actuated by the pureft motives, in oppofing that gentleman. He reprefented him as the author of the Maratta war; the caufe of the invafion of the Carnatic; and, of all the fubfequent miferies and diftreffes, to which that unhappy country has fo long been fubject. I was prefent too, in the gallery of the Houfe of Commons, when he fo folemnly pledged himfelf to God, the Houfe of Commons, and his country, to prove Mr. Haftings a moft notorious delinquent; and when he faid the world would be aftonifhed at a Report he was foon to bring forwards. I was fo much affected, Mr. Editor, with Mr. Burke's eloquent declamation, that I really wondered how any fet of men could be fo mad as to protect, for a moment, fuch a fhocking character as this Mr. Haftings appeared

peared to be. I watched with impatience the publication of Mr. Burke's Report; I read it with attention, but without finding proof of Mr. Haftings' delinquency; though, to be fure, it did appear to me that he had carried the power of patronage to an unwarrantable extent, in one inftance, as Mr. Burke ftated it. The appendix I had not then an opportunity of feeing, as it was not publifhed.

When this Mr. Scott's letters came out, I fent immediately to Sewell's for the pamphlet; I read them, and I muft declare to you, Mr. Editor, if what Major Scott advances is founded in truth, he has moft completely exculpated Mr. Haftings; but if he has mifreprefented any circumftance, I hope he will be punifhed with the utmoft feverity of the law. One point I can vouch for, that his quotations from the Appendix, which I have lately read, are very exact; and I wifh, Mr. Editor, the conduct of his Majefty's minifters would, at all times, bear fo fevere a fcrutiny as the conduct of Mr. Haftings has done, particularly in the article of the expenditure of public money.

I really

I really conceived, Mr. Editor, that Mr. Haſtings had ſent Mr. Scott to England, with a view of ſecuring him in the poſſeſſion of the government of Bengal, by *management*, a word of extenſive ſignification; but I find, upon enquiry, that Mr. Haſtings has invariably preſſed for a deciſion, without expreſſing much ſolicitude as to what it may be; and that Mr. Scott's ſole object has been to defend the character of Mr. Haſtings from the ungenerous attacks of men, who are eagerly waiting for appointments to the Supreme Council of India. I find too, upon enquiry, Mr. Editor, that ſuch is the opinion Mr. Haſtings's conſtituents have of his abilities, integrity, and honor, (and the Proprietors of India Stock are as independent men as any in this kingdom) that although the late miniſters were againſt him; although the Rockingham party, (formerly his firmeſt friends) and thirteen Directors, including the Chairman and his Deputy, were againſt him, yet their united and ſtrenuous endeavours, aided by Treaſury letters, could only produce ſeventy-five votes, out of five hundred and four, for his diſmiſſion; four hundred and twenty-eight voting for his continuance. A

majority

majority fo confiderable in his favor, muft neceffarily have had great weight, and will, I dare fay, induce every Member of the Houfe of Commons to examine and judge for himfelf in future; and not, as I am afraid was the cafe laft year, depend upon the judgment, the integrity, and the impartiality of Mr. Edmund Burke. Let me again obferve to you, Mr. Editor, that if Major Scott has dared to mifreprefent a fingle circumftance in his letters, he ought to be profecuted with the utmoft feverity of the law; if he has not, what reparation can the author of the Ninth Report make, for wantonly traducing the character of an abfent man?

Broad-ftreet,
July 29, 1783.   A CITIZEN.

LETTER II.

Mr. EDITOR,

I THANK you for your speedy insertion of my letter of the 29th ult.—and I feel so well pleased with being in print, for the first time these fifty years, that I may perhaps trouble you in future. I assure you, Mr. Editor, my attention has been very strongly drawn to the Ninth Report of the Select Committee.—Our Parliamentary orators have represented East Indians as little better than Devils upon earth, and I expected to find some proofs of the delinquency of the man Mr. Burke describes, as the first and most notorious of these plunderers: I mean Mr. Hastings. There is but one accusation against him in the Ninth Report, which appeared to bear hard upon him ; and that is what I hinted at in my last letter,—giving a contract to the son of Mr. Sulivan, the late Chairman of the Court of
Direc-

tors, upon improper terms.—To be sure, Mr. Editor, if this could have been proved, it would have funk Mr. Haftings in the opinion of every honeft man ; but, to my furprize and fatisfaction, I find this tranfaction fo fully explained, fo completely juftified from authentic records (unlefs the Appendix deceives me) that every honeft man on our fide Temple Bar, will pronounce Mr. Haftings exculpated from the charge of wafting the public money for private purpofes.

I have a very great refpect, Mr. Editor, for our moft excellent Conftitution.—But I do think it a misfortune, that it fhould be ftrictly conftitutional for a Committee of the Houfe of Commons to reprefent a man in high office, as a very bafe and unworthy character, and then to let the matter drop altogether ;—for in this Ninth Report it is obferved, " That the Committee do not bring " charges, though their Reports may furnifh " matter for charges." And further, " That " they are not obliged to report all they hear " or know upon a fubject."—" That it is at " the difcretion of the party accufed, to re " ply, or not, hereafter."—Why, what a

B   doctrine

doctrine is this, Mr. Editor ? What honest man, in future, can sleep in peace in his bed, who has had any transactions with the public ? He may be abused and scandalized, his cha- racter may be attacked, to answer a private purpose, as was really the case with Mr. Su- livan and Sir William James ;—and, after all, a Secretary of State may get up in the House, and say, the determination of his innocence must be postponed to a future day ; by these means leaving the malicious part of mankind to draw conclusions of the guilt of gentlemen who were ready and eager to prove their in- nocence. Now in the case of Mr. Hastings, to be sure, any man who reads the Ninth Re- port, will think him guilty : but let the same man read the Appendix, and Mr. Scott's let- ters, and he will pronounce, as I do, that Mr. Hastings has been basely, and scanda- loufly treated.

I have seen, Mr. Editor, in several of your papers, and indeed in other papers too, an account of the appointment of one William Burke, Esq; to the office of Receiver of the Balances due from the Company to the Crown in India. You have been so accurate as to

state

ſtate the different orders that were iſſued from hence, and the periods at which they were iſſued. Still, however, this affair appeared to me ſo extraordinary, that I could not give credit to it. That a man, who like Mr. Edmund Burke, had talked for many years of the neceſſity of public œconomy; who had even attacked the Civil Liſt; who interfered in the domeſtic arrangements of our moſt gracious Sovereign, God bleſs him! who had brought in a bill to aboliſh ſundry offices, by which very many worthy families are reduced to beggary and want: That ſuch a man, Mr. Editor, ſhould have created an uſeleſs office for his couſin, juſt to put three thouſand pounds a year into his pocket, and to take ſo much from the ſtate, was, to me, abſolutely incredible! I ſpoke to a brother citizen yeſterday, a very honeſt, worthy man, who is in the Direction. I aſked him if it was true, that William Burke, Eſq; was appointed Mr. Edmund Burke's Deputy in India; and if it was true that no ſuch appointment did exiſt, in the time of that profuſe Miniſter, Lord North, as Mr. Burke formerly deſcribed him? He told me, " It cer-
" tainly is ſo; no ſuch appointment did exiſt
" in

" in Lord North's time. I have examined
" the Records of the Company, and I find
" that *William Burke, Efq*; was appointed, by
" the Lords of the Treafury, Deputy to
" *Edmund Burke, Efq*; at the recommendation
" of the faid Edmund Burke, Efq; and that
" this appointment was notified to us by
" *Richard Burke, Efq*; a few days before the
" death of the Marquis of Rockingham ; and
" I can further tell you, my friend, that the
" appointment is worfe than ufelefs—it is
" mifchievous."—Really, Mr. Editor, I can
find no inftance like this, of a wafte of public
money for private purpofes, by Mr. Haftings,

Broad-ftreet,
Aug. 1, 1783.

A CITIZEN,

LETTER III.

Mr. EDITOR.

A Serious and attentive perusal of some late publications, excited my curiosity in a very great degree, to be fully informed of the conduct of our great men towards Mr. Haftings. Amongft us old fashioned folks in the city, he is a man, whofe extraordinary and perfevering character has attracted our particular attention. All people allow him to be a defpifer of money. I never heard of him foliciting a Peerage, or even the title of a Baronet of Great-Britain from any Minifter. He has neither family nor parliamentary intereft, nor has his agent Mr. Scott, attempted to force himfelf into the Lower Houfe, that he may meet Mr. Burke upon equal terms. Our city oracles fay, that Mr. Haftings poffeffes very great abilities, with uncommon application to bufinefs; and my

worthy

worthy friend the Director, tells me, that even his enemies in the India-Houfe, allow him to be a found politician, an able ftatef-man, and a fkilful financier. He added, even the croakers, who would perfuade us all was loft, have held down their heads abafhed and afhamed, fince we received the accounts of our late fucceffes, and the Marrata peace. I lately afked a friend of mine, who has four votes, and great intereft in the Proprietary, what would have been the confequence had Mr. Haftings been recalled in 1782? We fhould have loft India, he replied; a new Governor could not have raifed the fupplies, and our negociations with the Marratas muft have been fufpended. -As you wifh to be acquainted with our politics in Leadenhall-ftreet, I will give you a fhort hiftory of them. When Lord North laid violent hands upon the Company, in 1773, Mr. Haftings was the Governor of Bengal; it was thought prudent to continue him, but two Gentlemen powerfully connected, were fent out in the Council, and upon the breaking out of the difputes in Bengal, Lord North and his friends determined to remove Mr. Haftings; they procured a majority of one vote

amongft

amongſt the Directors, ſeveral of whom en-
joyed Government contracts, to ſecond their
views; but the Proprietors overſet the at-
tempts of the Miniſtry, and in this virtuous
ſtruggle, were even aſſiſted by the Duke of
Richmond, and all the good men of the
Rockingham party, who uſed to ſay in thoſe
days, that the Eaſt-India Company ought not
to be managed by John Robinſon. You and
I, my friend, have lived to ſee ſtrange altera-
tions. The two powerful men, General Cla-
vering and Colonel Monſon died ; then it
was that Lord North ſhewed a deſire to ſup-
port Mr. Haſtings; and tho' he had taken
much pains to remove him, in 1776, yet in
1780, and 1781, he was the very man who
propoſed him to be continued at the head of
the Government. See, my friend, how matters are carried on in this ſilly country; for
though Mr. Haſtings had committed no
crime, yet his former friend's, the Rocking-
hams, deſerted him the moment Lord North
took him up! Thus matters went on till
March, 1782. You remember with what ad-
vantages the Rockingham people then came
in, and in how high a light many of us in

the

the city held Edmund Burke, the panegyrift of that party. We were tired of the American war; we heard of nothing but defeats in all quarters. Many of our friends were fo far impofed upon, and led away by the inflammatory fpeeches of Mr. Fox and Mr. Burke, that we believed Lord North to be the moft extravagant, abandoned, and flagitious Minifter that this country had ever been curfed with. To be fure in thofe days, we never thought thefe three men could kifs and be friends in lefs than a year; fo ignorant we citizens are of high life!——We gave the new men credit for every thing they did, and every thing they faid; even Lord Rodney's recal and Mr. Burke's attack upon him, did not excite the popular refentment.; what then could the friends of Mr. Haftings expect? An abfent man; no family or parliamentary intereft; the falary of his office twenty-five thoufand pounds a year; a profpect opening of further removals; for Mr. Haftings once difpofed of, Mr. Hornby, Mr. Wheler, and Mr. Macpherfon would foon have followed: The falaries of thefe Gentlemen amounting to fixty one thoufand pounds a year, independent of the great power and patronage

patronage annexed to their offices. Think
my friend, what a temptation to the many
needy dependents of our great men, who
were themfelves, moſt of them, at leaſt, in
the greateſt diſtreſs, and in debt to every one
that would truſt them! Such a proſpect was,
indeed, enough to allure almoſt every gambler
at Brooks's, to the ſtandard of the Miniſter.
Two Committees ſitting, the virtuous Edmund Burke, and the immaculate General
Richard Smith, the leading members of one
of them. Popular prejudices ſtrong; what
then had the Miniſtry to fear? Victory was
ſecure ; they had only to fix the mode of attack. To be ſure there were ſome members
of the cabinet, to their eternal honor be it
ſpoken, who thought the long and faithful
ſervices of Mr. Haſtings, his ſpirit, and deciſion during the war, his relief of the Carnatic, and his wonderful exertions in every
part, deſerved a better return than a diſgrace-
ful and ignominious removal; but they were
borne down by the weight of the Rockingham
party, and compelled to ſubmit. The teme-
rity and preſumption of Mr. Haſtings's enemies did, what his great merits would not
otherwiſe have enabled him to do : it left him

to save India. The Ministers ordered the Directors to do, what the Proprietors in the end would not permit them to perform. If a Bill had been produced in May, 1782, Mr. Burke and his friends might have hurried it through in a month; but they had so completely silenced Lord North, who scarcely appeared, except in defence of Mr. Rigby, that they did not conceive any body of men would be hardy enough to dispute their pleasure, when it came forth in the form of a vote of the House of Commons. When this vote did pass, though the fate of India depended upon the wisdom of it, there were, fewer Members present, as our Epsom friend tells me, than generally attend a common Turnpike Bill. Mr. Johnstone told them then, that the vote would be nugatory if the Company differed from the House in opinion, as to the merits of Mr. Hastings; but Mr. Fox, and Mr. Burke, in the height of their power and populariy, treated this wholesome hint with disregard. "Who dare dispute a vote " of this House?" was the laconic reply, and the ministerial fiat was sent to the India House, where thirteen Directors, including the Chairs, were obedient to the mandate, But

now

now was the time, my friend, for Mr. Fox
and Mr. Burke to find, that they were not
quite fo powerful on this fide Temple-bar as
at Weftminfter. The independent Proprietors
who owed Mr. Haftings protection and
fupport, in return for long fervice, tried fi-
delity, and found integrity, in difficult and
tempting fituations, were determined to judge
for themfelves. The refult you know, and in
your next letter afk Mr. Fox, Mr. Burke,
and the thirteen Directors of their party,
if they do not think the Proprietors perform-
ed good fervice to their country and the Eaft-
India Company, when they preferved Mr.
Haftings in the government of Bengal.

Thefe, Mr. Editor, are my neighbour's fentiments, and his words, as nearly as I can re-
collect them. You fhall have my opinion in
another letter.

Broad ftreet,
Aug. 4, 1783.

A CITIZEN.

LETTER IV.

MR. EDITOR,

IN reading Mr. Scott's preface to his letters, I was a good deal ftruck, by the account he has given of Mr. Burke's moving for papers of fo old a date as 1776, to be laid before the Houfe of Commons, with a view of making the world fuppofe that Mr. Haftings had about that time been guilty of fome act of delinquency, or at leaft that a difcovery of former mifdeeds had then been made. We all of us know, Mr. Editor, how fturdily Mr. Burke ftood up in the Houfe of Commons, in defence of two men, whom four great lawyers had thought proper objects of a public profecution, and whom the late miniftry had folemnly difmiffed from their offices. The reafons affigned by Mr. Burke, for reftoring them to their ftations were " becaufe delinquency had not been proved a-

gainft

gainft them," and " that it would be hard to punifh men unconvicted of any crimes:"—Now, Mr. Editor, it was natural for me to enquire particularly what grounds Mr. Burke had for fuppofing Mr. Haftings to be a delinquent, nay, for afferting that he was one? Either thefe grounds muft be very ftrong, I faid to myfelf, or Mr. Burke muft be a very bad man—for in one inftance he reftores men to refponfible offices, againft whom there were the ftrongeft fufpicions of mal-practices, and in another cafe, he pofitively pronounces a Gentleman in high office, a notorious delinquent, previous to his even calling for the proofs. Indeed, Mr. Editor, the proofs ought to be very ftrong to juftify Mr. Burke, in ufing fuch language. Mr. Scott has already detected the falfe ftatement of the opinion of the feveral lawyers who were confulted, and he has proved from their own words, that inftead of advifing a profecution, as the Ninth Report ftates, they actually did the very reverfe. In looking over the appendix, I was much ftruck with the opinion of John Smith of Drapers Hall, the Company's Solicitor, a fhrewd, fenfible, long-headed man; and if he, Mr. Editor, gave fuch an opinion in 1776,

as

as I now copy from the Appendix to the
Ninth Report, No. 111, A. what, I afk
you, and through your means I defire to afk
Mr. Burke, can any Member of Parliament
make of thefe charges in the Autumn or
Winter of 1783?

   " Upon the whole of this evidence, I can-
" not bring myfelf to think, that there is
" fufficient ground for the Company to com-
" mence a fuit againft Mr. Haftings, for re-
" covery of thofe fums to which my obfer-
" vations are confined ; I mean all the fums
" ftated, except the lack and an half upon
" which the opinion of counfel has been
" taken. The proof is exceedingly con-
" fufed ; but when I confider the eagernefs
" the majority of the council have fhewn to
" eftablifh thofe charges ; *the extraordinary
" meafures they purfued for the purpofe*; the
" very eafy mode of proving the facts if
" true ; the very flender proof (if any), that
" is given, the obfervation arifing upon the
" face of the proof, and the flat contra-
" diction of Muny Begum; thefe various
" circumftances, on my mind, amount al-
" moft to *an abfolute conviction*, that the ftory
                 " *cannot*

" *cannot be true.* If the fact had been true,
" the persons mentioned by Nundcomar, as
" those through whose hands the first · four
" articles were paid, might have been ex-
" amined, and they must have proved the
" facts ; but it does not appear, that any one
" of them was called upon, although most
" of them were resident in Calcutta. This
" proof would have been easy and certain ;
" if any thing had been given for procuring
" the Naibship for Goordass, he must have
" known it ; but he was not asked a question
" upon that subject : The only witnesses
" that attempt any proof are Nundcomar,
" and his son-in-law Goordass. As to Nund-
" comar, if his bad character was not too
" well established, not to deserve credit, the
" manner in which he tells this story would
" destroy his credit. In the outset, he avows
" making those charges against Mr. Hastings,
" only because he feared complaints would
" be made against himself, and because he
" was angry at Mr. Hastings shewing disre-
" spect to him, and favour to others. He
" states the money all to have been paid,
" in August, September, October, and No-
" vember 1772 ; but the letter produced by
" him

" him, in confirmation of this ftory, is not
" pretended to be received till 1773, long
" after the payments are pretended to be
" made; yet the letter imports the requeft of
" a loan, to make a payment of One Hundred
" Thoufand Rupees. If Nundcomar had
" either paid or engaged to pay fuch large
" fums for Muny Begum, no doubt in the
" letter, he is fuppofed to have written to her,
" he would have informed her of it. I can-
" not help thinking that this letter was forg-
" ed."

Here, Mr. Editor, I have given you John
Smith's opinion. The fentiments of the
counfellors were equally honorable for Mr.
Haftings. The matter dropped; yet at this
diftance of time, Mr. Burke revives it. Indeed, indeed, Mr. Editor, thefe are fhameful proceedings. Is this to be one of the
bleffed effects of the coalition, that Lord
North fhall affift Mr. Burke in the perfecu-
tion of fo great a character as Mr. Haftings?
I cannot think fo favorably of Lord North's
conduct as Mr. Scott does; but I venture to
prophecy, Mr. Editor, that Edmund Burke
will be as unfuccefsful in attacking the character

racter and honeſt fame of Mr. Haſtings, as
he was in defending the men whom he re-
ſtored ſome time ago to their offices.

When I ſee ſuch ſcandalous doings going
forward, I cannot forbear ſpeaking out. If I
go to 'Change, to the London Tavern, or
the Queen's Arms, I meet nothing but long
faces: that we are a ruined nation all men
agree, and if Lord North, by his meaſures,
has not brought us to this ſad paſs, Mr. Fox
and Mr. Burke, by their oppoſition, have done
it. Who would have thought, Mr. Editor,
that after ſuch bitter enmity, theſe men could
have joined; for no other purpoſe than to
ſhare amongſt themſelves, and their depend-
ants, the little that is left! Here we ſee
Lord North with places for himſelf, his ſons,
couſins, and others, to a great amount. Then
again we behold Mr. Burke with places of
old ſtanding, or newly created, in the poſſeſſion of himſelf, his ſon, brother, and couſins, to the enormous amount, as I have ſeen
in print, of 25,500l. a year. Then again
Mr. Fox with his connections at the Treaſury,
Admiralty, &c.—Thus dividing the patronage of England amongſt them, and not con-

D tented

tented with that, we have feen Mr. Burke attacking in a fhameful manner, (as every man in the city allows, even the few friends that are left to Edmund Burke allow it) a man, who amidft all the ftruggle for places and power in this abandoned country, has proceeded in a fpirited and honorable difcharge of his duty, and has had the glory to fave India before he knew of the peace in Europe: That Mr. Burke from intereft, paffion, envy, and difappointment, fhould behave as he has done, it is not to be wondered at; but that Lord North fhould act the part of Noll Bluff to this Sir Jofeph, is indeed moft extraordinary!

A CITIZEN.

Broad-ftreet, 6th Auguft 1783.

LETTER

L E T T E R V.

MR. EDITOR,

I Dined yefterday with a friend in Surry, who has a feat in parliament, and in his parlour window lay the 10th report of the Select Committee. "" What the duce!" exclaimed I—" another report from that in- " duftrious, *impartial*, and indefatigable bo- " dy!"—" Yes," replied the Member, " and " a very fevere one too."—" I think quite " the contrary," faid my friend, the Proprietor, who was prefent: " I have read it with attention, but can find nothing in it to the difadvantage of Mr. Haftings: it will doubtlefs be completely anfwered; but as I have fome little knowledge of India matters, picked up by a conftant attendance at General Courts, reading all India pamphlets, and having, for a Bengal

cor-

correfpondent, a very intelligent young man, my nephew William; I could not read the Tenth Report without putting the reflections, that occurred at the time, upon paper, and they are at the fervice of my friend the Citizen, if he chufes to make them the fubject of his two next letters."——To be fure, Mr. Editor, I readily accepted his offer, and I hope the following account will be as acceptable to your numerous readers, as, I confefs to you, it was to me.

'Mr. Haftings has faid, and the truth
'of the obfervation will ftrike every man who
'attentively reads the Tenth Report, That
'there is no propofition which the wit of
'man can devife, which the wit of man can-
'not find plaufible, and perhaps even juft
'caufe of cenfure, by a falfe and partial re-
'view of it; and I, of all men, may be al-
'lowed to dread this treatment, after having
'invariably experienced it in every inftance
'of my public life.'

The Tenth Report is in fact the fpeech made by General Richard Smith, at a Court of Proprietors, on the 24th of October laft, enlarged

enlarged and improved. I remember the
General told us then, that though we would
not hear him, he would take care to be heard
in another place; and I was prefent when he
made his complaint in Parliament, that he
was interrupted by clamour by the Proprietors, though unluckily he forgot to ftate that
he was heard for upwards of an hour with
great attention; it is true, the Court would
not patiently attend to a fecond Philippic
from him, on the fame day. The Report
ftates what the General then faid, that Mr.
Haftings went up to Benares, with a view of
getting fifty lacks of rupees, for the Company, from Cheyt Sing; but being difap-
pointed, he perfuaded the Vizier to feize the
treafures of his mother, for the Company's
fervice, under the pretence of his having le-
vied troops for Cheyt Sing at the time of his
revolt, through her eunuchs, Jewar Ally
Cawn, and Behar Ally Cawn. The General
ludicroufly compared thefe men, and their
efforts, to Pachierotti and Tenducci, exciting
a revolt in London ——This is the outline
of General Richard Smith's fpeech on that
day of triumph for Mr. Haftings, and it is
the outline of the Tenth Report too. In the
Re-

Report, as in the speech, there are many artful
appeals to the passions and prejudices of the
moment; but the suspected compiler of it has
at last talked himself out of all credit. Indeed his professions and his actions are proved
to have been so far at variance, that men will,
in future, examine for themselves, and not
take for matter of fact, the sublime rapsodies
of the person who protected two public de-
faulters, and prosecuted Lord Rodney and
Mr. Hastings ;—who from being the calum-
niator, is become the panygerist of Lord
North,—and who earnestly recommending
œconomy when out of place, was the person
to solicit the establishment of a sinecure
office, when in place, for the emolument of
a near relation. The people of England
having, by sad misfortune, recovered their
sober senses, and seeing how miserably they
were disappointed when they trusted to the
flowery professions of Mr. Burke;————
perhaps the following plain narration
of authentic facts may now be opposed,
with success, to the splendid misrepresenta-
tions contained in the Tenth Report. I
find, by my nephew William's letters, that
the late Vizier died in the month of
January,

January, 1775, and that he w asfuppofed
to leave behind him above two million
fterling, in fpecie and jewels, befides other
valuable effects.——Thefe, as is the cuftom of the Eaft, were lodged for fecurity in
the Zenana, or womens apartments; and by
that means fell into the hands of the Begum,
the wife of the Vizier. When Affolph ul
Dowlah fucceeded his father, he found a
large army greatly in arrears, clamorous, and
mutinous for want of pay, and he himfelf de-
prived of his father's treafures, which of right
belonged to him, was unable to fatisfy their
juft demands. The prefence of the Englifh
army faved his life more than once.——Fre-
quent applications were made to the old
woman, the mother of Affolph ul Dowlah,
for his father's treafures, but without fuccefs.
In October, 1775, Mr. John Briftow went to
Fyzabad, and he writes to the Supreme Council, Appendix, No. 1, " that in explaining
" particularly to the Begum, in writing,
" how impoffible it was for the Nabob to
" conduct his government without further
" affiftance. I further infinuated to her, that
" the treafures fhe poffeffed, were the *trea-*
" *fures of the ftate,* as fhe had not *fucceeded*
" to

" to them by any *legal right*, and that they
" had been hoarded up to provide *again? an*
" *emergency.*"

After some negociation, the old woman
consented to pay thirty lacks of rupees, on
condition Mr. Briftow would engage, on the
part of the Company, that no further demands should be made upon her.—This he
was obliged to consent to, without waiting for
inftructions from the Supreme Council ; and
they approved the meafure, fince it was abfo-
lutely neceffary.——There were feveral difputes between the Begum's Eunuchs and the
Vizier's Minifter, relative to the nature of the
effects which were paid in part of the thirty
lacks ; and the Begum herfelf wrote a very
violent letter to Mr. Haftings, on part of
which Mr. Francis makes the following obfervation, " I cannot conceive fhe (the Be-
" gum) has the leaft right to interfere in the
" Nabob's government. In a country where
" women are not allowed a free agency, in
" the moft trifling domeftic affairs, it feems
" extraordinary that this lady fhould prefume
" to talk of appointing Minifters, and go-
" verning kingdoms. Upon the whole, I
" look

" look upon the letter as not of her writing,
" who probably cannot read, but as the com-
" pofition of fome of her fervants ; perhaps
" of the *Eunuch* who brings it."

The Begum's complaints were fent to Mr.
Briftow, and his obfervations upon them will
perhaps throw as much light upon the real
character of the Begum, and her Eunuchs, as
the committee's reflections on Lieutenant Colonel Harpur's evidence, who quitted Bengal
ten years ago, and before the death of Sujah
Dowlah, which event made the Eunuchs of
confequence in Oude.

Mr. Briftow fays, " In making this com-
" plaint, the Begum forgets the improper
" conduct of her own fervants, who have hi-
" therto preferved a *total independence of the*
" *Nabob's authority*, beat the officers of his go-
" vernment, and *refufed obedience to his Pere-*
" *wannahs.*——The Begum's Eunuchs did
" induftrioufly fpread reports of Murteza
" Cawn's ill intentions, to break into the
" Zenana, and feize all the effects and money
" that could be found,—The Begum had
" great intereft in the late Vizier's time.

E   " On

" On the Nabob's acceffion, he at once placed
" the fole management in the hands of Mur-
" teza Cawn, which difgufted both her and
" her adherents, *particularly their Eunuchs*,
" *who have their views in keeping the wealth in*
" *the Begum's poffeffion.* The principal, Bahar
" Ally Cawn *enjoys her entire confidence.*" Mr.
Briftow fends the Supreme Council, with thefe
remarks, a letter from the Begum to him,
which concludes thus, " Caufe the 56 lacks
" to be reftored to me ; do not you then take
" any part in the affair, and then let Affolph
" ul Dowla, and Murteza Cawn, in *whatever*
" *manner they are able, take fums of money from*
" *me. They will then fee the confequences.*"

You fhall have the remainder of my
friend's remarks, Mr. Editor, in another
letter.

Broad-ftreet,
Aug. 10, 1783.

A CITIZEN.

L E T T E R VI.

Mr. Editor,

I Now fend you the remainder of my friend
the Proprietor's account.

" The agreement between the Vizier and
his mother, to which Mr. Briftow, on the
part of the Company, was guarantee, was ex-
ecuted on the 15th of October, 1775, but it
was not until the 7th of July, 1776, that fhe
paid the balance, or gave affignments, and
then the Vizier was obliged to fubmit to a
confiderable deduction from the fum fpeci-
fied in the original treaty. And Mr. Briftow
obferved to the fupreme Council, " the Be-
" gum can make no great claim on the Com-
" pany for protection, *when fhe herfelf has in-*
" fringed the conditions of the treaty, of which
" they were the guarantees." In the fame letter,

ter, dated 3d of January, 1776, Mr. Briſtow
ſays, "How far ſhe (the Begum) may be
" better affected to the Engliſh than the Na-
" bob, I leave to the conſideration of the
" Honorable Board, from the following fact.
" On the concluſion of the treaty between
" the Company and the Nabob, the Begum
" blamed his Excellency very highly, and
" inſiſted on his not ceding Benares, offering
" *of perſelf* a ſum of money in lieu of it."—
Mr. Briſtow writes to the Begum in reply to
a letter of complaint from her. " With re-
" ſpect to your Highneſs jaghiers, the Nabob
" agrees to one method, which is, that you
" give them up entirely, and inſtead thereof
" receive a monthly ſtipend, through the
" channel of any perſon you chooſe to fix on;
" for the Nabob obſerved to me, *that two*
" *rulers were too much for one country.* By
" this propoſal, the Nabob is deſirous of pro-
" moting your Highneſs' quiet, tranquillity,
" and ſatisfaction. The Nabob ſays that in
" this caſe you will have no vexation, and
" will conſtantly receive your ſtipend with-
" out trouble."

This

This extract proves that the idea of re-
suming the Begum's jaghier was entertained
as early as 1776 by the Vizier, and not, as is
insinuated in the report, mentioned to him
for the first time in 1781, by Mr. Haftings.

The Vizier however could not procure his
mother's confent, to accept an annual fum
in lieu of her jaghier, and her Eunuchs were
in poffeffion of very great power and influence, till the time of Cheyt Sing's revolt. Her
activity in his behalf, is proved beyond the
poffibility of a doubt—Her difaffection, and
the intrigues of her Eunuchs were equally
well proved. Was not Mr. Haftings, under
fuch circumftances, ftrictly juftifiable in with-
drawing our guarantee, and by that means
enabling the Vizier to poffefs himfelf of thofe
treafures which were his undoubted right,
and which were to be applied to the preffing
exigencies of the Eaft-India Company?
However pathetically Mr. Edmund Burke
may talk of thefe matters, his pretended humanity will no longer deceive in the City;
and my nephew, William, affured me in one
of his laft letters, that we owe the preferva-
tion

tion of India, to the confiderable fum of feven hundred thoufand pounds, which we received from the Vizier in February 1782;
that he could not have paid this money, except from the hoarded treafures of his de-
ceafed father, and thofe ought to have been
in his poffeffion many years ago, fince the
Begum, had not the fmalleft right to retain
them.——This is the true ftate of a tranfaction, which the ingenuity of the compiler
of the tenth report, has turned and twifted fo
as to bewilder a man of common underftand-
ing. An old lady immured by cuftom in a
feraglio for life, was permitted by us, to retain a large treafure, the property of her
fon; fhe employs this money, and her exten-
five influence, in oppofition to the Britifh
government—She is compelled in confequence to relinquifh the treafure—no further
violence is offered, nor are her Eunuchs ill
treated, though well deferving an exemplary
punifhment. Leaft the term Eunuch fhould
infpire my worthy fellow citizens with the
idea of a poor, miferable, fqueaking, Italian
ballad finger, I will copy an account of a
difturbance excited by an Eunuch in Oude,

as it was fent to me by my nephew William, in 1776.

Cojee Buffaun a *complete Eunuch*, was the favorite general of Sujah Dowlah, and very well known to General Smith and Sir Robert Barker. His influence at the court of Oude was confiderably leffened by the death of Sujah Dowlah, though he was continued by his fucceffor at the head of a large body of his forces, He was jealous of Murteza Cawn, the favorite minifter of Affolph ul Dowlah, and was fuppofed to have entered into engagements with Saudut Ally and the Begum, for the depofition of the Nabob, and the deftruction of his minifter. In December, 1775, Cojee Buffaun, according to a pre-concerted plan, invited the minifter, Murteza Cawn, to an etertainment with feveral of his principal friends. The Company drank hard, the dancing girls were called in, and, after a little time, Murteza Cawn, the prime minifter, was carried in a ftate of intoxication into another room, and there inhumanly murdered.—After perpetrating this fhocking act, Cojee Baffaun, with his fword drawn, rufhed into the prefence of the Vizier, and was advancing

vancing towards his perfon, either to feize him, or to put him to death.—Buffaun had drank hard himfelf, and betrayed fuch ftrong marks of confufion in his countenance, that the Vizier with great prefence of mind called out " Will no one rid me of this traitor?"— twenty fwords were drawn, and in an inftant Cojee Buffaun was cut to pieces. Saudut Ally fled with a few of his confidential attendants, nor were the parties concerned in the plot ever difcovered; fo far is clear, Murteza Cawn, the Vizier's prime minifter was murdered by the Eunuch, Cojee Buffaun, who was himfelf put to death by the Vizier's attendants.—I relate this fact to prove that Eunuchs in India are bold, intriguing, and enterprifing men, nor was it right in General Smith to attempt to miflead us, by comparing them to Pachioretti and Tenducci; he knew better, though fome of us perhaps did not.

In the tenth report there are fome remarks upon a tranfaction, which I thought could not be related to the difcredit of Mr. Haftings. He received a prefent of ten lacks of rupees from the Vizier and his minifters, and told

told the Company of it. He received other presents, to the amount of nine lacks more, making in all one hundred and ninety thousand pounds sterling. This large sum he has paid into the Company's treasury. He does not even touch a farthing of the interest of it, instead of retaining the principal, which would have enabled him to vye with the gamblers at Brooks's, to be ranked as a companion for princes of the blood royal of France, and to have procured himself and a few of his friends, seats in a certain assembly, at the *next general election*, by bribery. The compiler of the tenth report has had wit and ingenuity enough to find out that " when " these facts become known in India, it is to " be feared that the servants of the Company " will be inclined to lessen their reverence " and respect to those acts of parliament " which were made to restrain them in pur- " suit of wealth ; and that they will be apt " to reconcile to their own minds, any devia- " tion from a strict obedience, by quoting " the example of the Governor-General, as " a rule by which they may guide their own " conduct !"

F

I con-

I conceive it impoffible that a tranfaction fo honorable to Mr. Haftings in every point of view, can operate to the difadvantage of the ftate, unlefs indeed, the fervants of the Company feeing that a man who has ferved faithfully and honeftly for above three and thirty years, and when he has every reafon to believe his fervice is drawing towards a clofe, candidly declares that he has received prefents to the amount of one hundred and ninety thoufand pounds, and accounts to the public treafury for every fhilling of the principal and intereft; if fuch a man, inftead of receiving from his conftituents a part of this fum, a life intereft in a part of it, or even the moft trifling mark of approbation, fhall have the mortification to be abufed for fo fingular an act of difintereftednefs and integrity ; if this tranfaction fhall be mifreprefented without doors, and be the fubject of a parliamentary Report; if that Report fhall be prefented to the Houfe of Commons by a man who ferved in Bengal four years and feven months only, in a ftation inferior to Mr. Haftings, but who was permitted by the Court of Directors to retain a prefent to the amount of thirty-fix

thoufand

thoufand pounds, although he actually made
the Company pay for all the prefents he
made in his public character, to the amount
of above fixteen thoufand pounds, and re-
tained in his own hands thofe he received in
return ; if, I fay, the fervants of the Company obferve, how unequally rewards, and
commendations are conferred upon different
men, as the fpirit of party, rather than that
of juftice prevails; then, and then only, can
this honorable act of the Governor-General
operate to the difadvantage of the ftate, by in-
ducing theCompany's fervants in India to believe, that no rectitude of conduct can fcreen
them from the malignant invectives of party malice, patriotic fpleen, and interefted
mifreprefentation."

Thefe, Mr. Editor, are my friend's remarks,
I will give you my homely fentiments in
another Letter.

Broad-ftreet, Auguft 11, 1783.

A CITIZEN.

LETTER VII.

MY good friend and neighbour, the Proprietor, called upon me laſt night, with ſome further remarks upon the Tenth Report, which I now tranſcribe, not doubting but that you and your Readers will be amuſed and inſtructed by them.

"I cannot help noticing a very curious aſſertion contained in the Tenth Report: "That the deciſion of the Court of Directors, as to the ten lacks of Rupees given by the Vizier and his Miniſter to Mr. Haſtings was very unjuſt." It appears to me that theſe five or ſix *virtuous* Reporters (not poſſeſſing among them a ſhilling of property in India-ſtock) would perſuade the Court of Directors to return this money, becauſe they repreſent the Vizier to be a vaſſal of the Company's

pany's. Surely neither the Chairman, Sir
Henry Fletcher, nor any of the Directors, will
permit one or two men behind the curtain to
manage the affairs of the East-India Company. If any person should propose, either
in a Court of Directors, or in a Committee
of Correfpondence, to fend orders to the
Governor-General and Council, to pay back
these ten lacks of Rupees to the Vizier, we
should be at no lofs to guefs from what quar-
ter that person, bringing forward fuch a propofition, was advifed and directed; but
should a fingle Director adopt the ideas of
the Select Committe, after having given orders feveral months ago upon the fubject,
which were highly proper (becaufe they do
not preclude the East-India Company from
rewarding hereafter the important fervices of
Mr. Haftings) I hope there will be firmnefs
enough in a majority of the Directors to re-
fift the propofition. If we are to adopt this
wild idea of Mr. Burke, let us act confiftent-
ly. That gentleman's humanity is fo fub-
fervient to his party views, that from him
partial juftice only can be expected: but let
me afk General Richard Smith, if the Em-
peror Shaw Allum, the King of the world,

was

was not a vassal of the Company, and as poor
as any king upon earth, when the General accepted presents from him? Why not require
the General to return them all? I believe the
cash would be very acceptable to his Ma-
jesty, for my nephew William, writes me,
that from the time he quitted the English,
he has suffered the greatest distress. Why
not order the Company to pay his arrears of
tribute, for we have some patriots amongst us,
who say we had no right to withhold it?
Why not pay back to the poor distressed
unhappy Nabob of Arcot, some of the money that the Company has taken from him?
and why not call upon many English gentlemen to refund the presents they have received
from him? Let us, for God's sake, be a-
mused with no more of these rapsodies;
Mr. Hastings is not a man to make use of
unfair means to procure presents to himself;
he has too much spirit, and too great a disregard for money to obtain it by improper
means; if the Company thinks proper to
retain every shilling of the money received,
amounting to 190,000£. for their own use,
let them do it; they have a right to it; but
let not the ingenuity of Edmund Burke per-
suade

fuade the Chairman or any other Director of his party, that we fhall be difgraced, if we do not pay to the Vizier and his Minifter, the ten lacks of Rupees which they gave to Mr. Haftings in September, 1781. I believe there is not a more diftreffed Prince in India, than the Raja of Tanjore; why not call upon the family of the Burkes to refund all that they have received from him ? and, to complete with equity, this fyftem of reformation, let us fend tranfports from this country, let us embark every Englifhman in India, and let us in future appear there in the character of traders only. If we are not already fick of the Utopian fchemes of Edmund Burke, let us give the world a fure proof of our moderation. Having loft America, let us abandon India. I remember the time when General Richard Smith poffeffed a very large property in India-ftock, and when he wifhed to be thought the protector of the rights of the Eaft-India Company. He has now fold out even his fingle vote, has declared we are not folvent, and has exerted himfelf by every poffible means in his power, both in and out of Parliament, to remove Mr. Haftings.——

Surely

Surely, neither Mr. Fox, or any other Minister will think of defiring the Directors to employ a perfon in future, who has been fo hoftile to us."

Here, Mr. Editor, I have given you my friend's account at length.—I am a blunt citizen, but in my opinion it is very curious that the Select Committee fhould fix upon Mr. Haftings's prefents as the only ones that ought to be returned. To be fure, Mr. Editor, it is very generous of Mr. Burke and General Smith, to difpofe of other people's money as they do, I wifh I could fee them give up a little of their own with all my heart: a plain man like me muft wonder how this money bufinefs can be a proper object of enquiry for a Committee inftructed to *enquire into the ftate of the judicature in Bexgal,* and how the *Britifh poffeffions* in India may be beft governed."——The Court of Proprietors are much obliged to thefe gentlemen for their laudable zeal, and I hope, in return, they will appoint William Burke, Efq; the Tanjore agent, a Supreme Counfellor ; and General Smith, to the government of Bombay.

As

(49)

As you may not hear from me again for a month or two, Mr. Editor, I cannot avoid copying, for the edification of your readers, a few lines from a very extraordinary book juſt publiſhed, entitled, *The Life of Mr. Fox,*—
" But the public was peculiarly charmed and
" ſtruck with admiration, by the generous
" and diſintereſted patriotiſm of Mr. Burke,
" &c. &c. &c."—I will not ſurfeit you by a longer extract, but I wiſh to know if Edmund Burke's coalition with Lord North, and ſecuring to himſelf and his family 25,500l. a year, are proofs either of diſintereſtedneſs or patriotiſm?——If by the Public, the writer means the Citizens of London, or the People of England, I believe, Mr. Editor, they deem all Patriots in the Miniſtry, men of words and not of deeds, having been ſo groſsly duped and deceived by the very beſt of them.

Broad-ſtreet,
Aug. 18, 1783.

A CITIZEN.